UNDER PRESSURE

How to Handle Discrimination and Prejudice

by Catherine Chambers

W
FRANKLIN WATTS

First published in 2014 by Franklin Watts

Copyright © Arcturus Holdings Limited

Franklin Watts
338 Euston Road
London NW1 3BH

Franklin Watts Australia
Level 17/207 Kent Street, Sydney NSW 2000

Produced by Arcturus Publishing Limited,
26/27 Bickels Yard, 151–153 Bermondsey Street, London SE1 3HA

The right of Catherine Chambers to be identified as the author of this work has been asserted by her
in accordance with the Copyright, Designs and Patents Act 1988.

Editors: Rachel Minay and Joe Harris
Design: Emma Randall
Cover design: Emma Randall

Picture Credits
Corbis: 9 (Peter Dench/In Pictures); Shutterstock: cover (ostill), 3 (O Driscoll Imaging), 5 (Christy
Thompson), 7 (Leah-Anne Thompson), 8 (auremar), 10 (Monkey Business Images), 11 (Dasha
Petrenko), 12 (conejota), 13 (oliveromg), 14 (Martin Allinger), 15 (Radoslaw Lecyk), 16 (Ron Ellis), 17
(Dmitry Kalinovsky), 18 (Gladskikh Tatiana), 19 (CREATISTA), 20 (Martin Allinger), 21 (Darrin Henry), 22
(SeanPavonePhoto), 23 (Elena Elisseeva), 24 (michaeljung), 25 (lev radin), 26 (Michel Borges), 27 (Lisa
S.), 28 (michaeljung), 29 (kataijudit), 30 (wavebreakmedia), 31 (Lisa F. Young), 32 (Nagel Photography),
33 (Shots Studio), 34 (michaeljung), 35 (holbox), 36 (Monkey Business Images), 37 (Kzenon), 38
(Patricia Marks), 39 (Masson), 40 (photomak), 41 (oliveromg), 42 (Goodluz), 43 (spirit of america).

A CIP catalogue record for this book is available from the British Library.

Dewey Decimal Classification Number 303.3'85

ISBN 978 1 4451 3239 6

Printed in China

Franklin Watts is a division of Hachette Children's Books, an Hachette UK company.
www.hachette.co.uk

SL004069UK

Supplier 29, Date 0514, Print Run 3392

CONTENTS

WHAT ARE DISCRIMINATION AND PREJUDICE?

Discrimination means treating people differently, usually in a negative way. It stems from prejudice, which means having unfair opinions about someone or a group of people. These opinions are not based on actual evidence.

People may **shun** others they feel are different to them.

UNDER PRESSURE FROM PREJUDICE

If people hold prejudices against you and discriminate in favour of others, you will probably feel that this is very wrong. You may feel angry, upset, confused, lonely and isolated. You might not understand why people are treating you badly and feel the need to find ways of coping.

UNDER PRESSURE TO SHOW PREJUDICE

People will often try to influence you to be prejudiced against others. This puts you under a different kind of pressure. You might want to find ways of resisting this pressure in a positive way. This can mean challenging the views of narrow-minded friends or seeking out friends who have an open attitude towards difference. It can mean finding out more about the lives of others, so that you can better understand what it's like to be them.

Under Pressure Q&A

How can I make my friends understand?

My oldest friend and the best friend in the world comes from a difficult family. Her brother's been excluded from school and he's in trouble with the police. My other friends don't want me to talk to her, but I think that's mean. What do I do?

There is often a lot of pressure to discriminate against people. Explain all the wonderful things about your oldest friend to your other friends. Remind them that she is a person in her own right and that no one should be defined by the actions of her or his family. If they carry on being prejudiced, you might need to think hard about the value of their friendship.

THE IMPACT OF DISCRIMINATION AND PREJUDICE

Individuals who discriminate and show prejudice can cause serious upset to others. However, when many people discriminate, the result is much worse. People end up socializing only with others like themselves, and shunning other groups. Prejudice makes people wary of each other and can ruin relationships.

Is the police officer picking on this teenager? Or has this teenager shown unlawful prejudice against someone? Both are unfair.

WHAT IS STEREOTYPING?

Stereotyping means holding rigid ideas about particular groups of people. Some of these ideas are very old **assumptions**. They are often based on suspicion and rumour rather than fact. Stereotyping can lead to prejudice and discrimination.

Some people believe that all teenagers hanging out together cause trouble. This is a form of stereotyping.

ARE PEOPLE STEREOTYPING YOU?

If you think that people are stereotyping you, it might make it hard to socialize normally and make friends. It might even make you want to shun your own background and family. Remember, you have a right to join in without losing your own **identity**.

DISCUSSING STEREOTYPING IN SCHOOL

If stereotyping is happening in school, suggest to a teacher that you make it a subject for a debate. You could start by discussing something light-hearted and jokey, such as 'People who like video games are shy and boring. Does this statement stereotype gamers?' But follow the debate with a discussion on other types of stereotyping. If stereotyping seems to be getting out of hand, speak to a trusted teacher or school counsellor, or the school's buddying team if there is one.

Listen to what people say about themselves before you take notice of what others say about them.

DO YOU STEREOTYPE OTHERS?

Don't automatically pick out differences between yourself and others. Focus on their personal qualities. You can take an interest in someone's background but understand that this is not the most important thing about them. Knowing a broad range of people prepares you for life outside your small circle.

'Their parents thought I wouldn't be allowed'

I'm a Muslim girl and most days I go to mosque class after ordinary school. My school friends hang out at each other's houses after school and I wanted to come too. I could join them after mosque class. But their parents assumed I wouldn't be allowed because — supposedly — all Muslims are very strict. Well, that's not true. In fact it's a real stereotype! Fortunately my mum chatted to my friend's mum at a craft club. Mum said how lovely it would be if her daughter and others came round to my house after mosque class. So now we all hang out together and they know I like to have way too much fun!

WHAT IS SCAPEGOATING?

Scapegoating means blaming problems you see around you on an individual or a group of people. It is unfair and it is based on prejudice and stereotyping. Scapegoating is common because it gives a simple explanation for complex problems.

Fight back against negative stereotypes and scapegoating! You can use social media to give your side of the story.

COMMON TARGETS FOR SCAPEGOATING

Some groups are often scapegoated for the problems in our society. For example, immigrants to a country are often blamed for taking jobs and housing away from people who have been born there. People from poor areas or the young are often blamed for crime or dirty, litter-strewn streets. These social problems are very complex, and scapegoating just gets in the way of finding lasting solutions.

Young, single mothers are often scapegoated for social problems.

ARE YOU BEING SCAPEGOATED?

If you are facing scapegoating, try to find out exactly why you are being blamed. Are those targeting you only doing so because of prejudice against, for example, your age, **ethnic group** or family situation? Speak to a teacher, school counsellor or other trusted adult to get some advice on how to deal with this situation.

THINK FOR YOURSELF

Be wary of stories in the media that target particular groups. The media sometimes scapegoats people because it makes a good story, but the story may not be telling the whole truth.

Under Pressure Q&A

Can I do anything to stop it?

My two older sisters are both teenage mums. One of them is looking after her baby full-time, but the other is back at college now. Recently people have been shouting out as they go past our house. They're say that we are lazy **scroungers** who don't want to work. I think it's adults doing it. My mum's ignoring it, but it frightens me. Can I do anything?

The people shouting abuse are cowards, and your mum is being smart by ignoring them. However, if the problem doesn't get any better, you could speak to your mum about contacting your community policing team. They are trained to deal with this type of situation. Meanwhile, be proud of your family.

11

DISCRIMINATION AND BULLYING

People can suffer many forms of bullying as a result of discrimination. They might face social isolation, harmful gossip or even physical attacks. Victims of discrimination can suffer extreme loneliness, anger, **depression**, **anxiety** and low **self-esteem**. Young people can find it difficult to make friends and achieve at school.

SOCIAL ISOLATION AND HARMFUL GOSSIP

Social isolation means cutting someone out of normal life. He or she is ignored, shunned and excluded from social groups and activities. Those who are discriminating in this way sometimes spread gossip about their victims, too, often using social media to share abusive texts or post harmful messages about their victims.

PHYSICAL HARM

Discrimination can also lead to physical violence. If this has happened to you, you must tell a parent, carer, community police officer or school counsellor straight away. Violence is **illegal**. Victims are often afraid to speak out, but this is the first step towards discussing why you are facing discrimination and the first step towards making it stop.

Prejudice can lead to bullying and vandalism such as damaging property or writing graffiti.

DEALING WITH DISCRIMINATORY BULLYING

If you are being bullied as a result of discrimination, explain calmly that there is no reason why differences between you should lead to bullying. Point out the positive things you share. Most of all, remember there is never an excuse for bullying and you should not put up with it. Tell an adult what is happening or phone a helpline for advice.

REBUILD YOUR SELF-ESTEEM

Bullying can seriously affect a young person's self-esteem, especially if the bullies are targeting you because of prejudice against an aspect of your identity. While the bullying is being dealt with, rebuild your self-esteem by spending time with your family and supportive, like-minded friends.

Bullying based on prejudice against, for example, someone's background, can be particularly hurtful.

'I got caught up in something horrible'

This is very serious because I got caught up in something horrible. There's a girl in my class who me and my friends talked to sometimes because she seemed nice. Then we found out that she'd had **bulimia**, so we decided to ignore her. We called her 'disgusting' and 'greedy' and things like that, which I know now was really awful. Then it got worse, because we started texting and blogging about her. The girl's dad went mad and called the school and we got **suspended** for a week. I've learnt a bit more about illnesses like bulimia now and I've apologized to the girl, but I still feel ashamed that I was part of something so mean.

RACIAL DISCRIMINATION

Racial discrimination is one of the world's biggest problems. It can ruin people's lives and divide societies. **Racism** is the belief that some ethnic groups are better than others or the dislike of people of a certain race or people from a certain country. Racism is the result of prejudice and stereotyping.

THE IMPACT OF RACISM

Racial discrimination can range from verbal insults and damage to property to physical attacks. Racism is shameful and causes deep hurt and resentment. It can bring fear to ordinary activities, such as walking down a street, going to school, playing in the park, shopping or hanging out with friends. Racism often stops victims from mixing with other groups, which divides societies even more.

RACIAL STEREOTYPING

Racial discrimination is often based on ethnic stereotypes. Wrongly, some groups are stereotyped, for example as criminals, or poor at science, or only good at sport or music. Newcomers to a country are not the only targets of racial discrimination. In some countries, racism continues to hurt the original inhabitants or groups that have lived there for centuries.

Mixing with others is the best way to explore our similarities and respect our differences.

TACKLING RACISM

Racism is based on ignorance. If you are facing racial prejudice, try tackling it with the help of friends. Show surprise at the attitudes of those who are prejudiced against you – tell them the world has moved on. Point them to online movements, such as Youth Against Racism in Europe, that help explain why racism is wrong. If you continue to suffer racial prejudice or discrimination, you need to speak to a trusted adult. In some cases, it may be a matter for the police.

Festivals such as Chinese New Year celebrate the wide variety of races in modern cities.

Under Pressure Q&A

How should I answer them?

I was born in Syria, though I can't remember living there. Mum and Dad left there years ago to work here. They're doctors. But because of stuff in the news, some kids at school keep calling me a hopeless **refugee** and saying that I'm lucky to be here. I tell them I'm not a refugee, but then I feel bad for all the people who are. How should I answer them?

These students are using a lazy stereotype. Of course there would be nothing wrong with being a refugee, but it can be frustrating to be lumped together with others purely because of your nationality. Don't let them see that you are frustrated. Explain to them calmly that what they're saying makes no sense. Tell them that you deserve to be treated as an individual.

RELIGIOUS DISCRIMINATION

There can be a lot of fear and suspicion around unfamiliar religious beliefs, ceremonies and dress codes. This can lead to discrimination against people of different faiths and it can divide communities. We need to try to respect religious differences and treat members of all religions equally.

Find out about the different places of worship in your neighbourhood. Many are beautiful buildings.

FAITH COMMUNITIES

Religious groups are communities with shared beliefs and traditions. Some outsiders resent these communities because they feel excluded, and have confused or stereotyped views about their beliefs. However, most faith communities open their doors to groups wanting to know more about their beliefs. You could find out about groups in your own community and get to know more about your neighbours.

RELIGION AND THE MEDIA

Media headlines often highlight religious conflict around the world. This increases ignorance, fear and suspicion. Media organizations boost their ratings by reporting religious **extremism** and often distort the facts. For example, 93 per cent of Muslims worldwide reject extremism. But the media hardly ever reports this. Make sure you get your facts straight about faiths.

This Sikh teenager is proud of her family and her heritage.

BREAK DOWN BARRIERS

If you are facing prejudice about your religion, don't put up with it. Tell a trusted adult. With friends, try to set up a group with members of all faiths and those who have none. Discuss the beliefs you share, especially the caring and sharing side. Invite people to religious festivals, too. Explain their meaning and share the food and fun – this is a great way to break down barriers.

'They didn't let me join in'

I'm a Sikh boy and I have to wear my hair long and tied in a knot at the back of my head. We call it a patka. When I started secondary school, a lot of the boys started calling me a girl. They didn't let me join in when they played football at break time. I think that's really wrong. So I joined the football club after school on Wednesday and then those boys saw how well I could play. After a few long weeks, they started letting me join in at break. Some of them still call my patka stupid names, but I'm working on that!

HOME LIFE

There are many different types of family structure, but not all types are accepted in the same way. Many people regard the most stable type of family to be one where children live with their biological parents. This means that single-parent families are often labelled as unstable. Large families and children who are adopted or fostered can also face prejudice.

SINGLE-PARENT FAMILIES

Children of single parents are often stereotyped as **disruptive** and unhappy. Single parents who choose to stay at home may be accused of not wanting to find a job, while those who work can be accused of leaving their children 'home alone' or letting them 'run wild'.

LARGE FAMILIES

Some people stereotype very large families with lots of children. It is often assumed that the parents do not work to pay for their children's care – that they rely on public money. Some people think that each child in a large family cannot possibly be treated as an individual or given enough time with his or her parents.

The media often picks on large families, especially where the parents are poor.

FIGHT WITH FACTS

If your family is being stereotyped, talk to people about the real facts. Studies show that most children raised in single-parent families are happy, confident and no more likely to 'run wild' than children with two parents at home. Most parents with a lot of children are hard-working and their children have no problems around their individual identity. Children who are being fostered or have been adopted are often stereotyped as being insecure. However, adopted children are no more insecure than those living with birth parents, while those who are fostered in a stable, caring environment have happy futures.

Studies show that children are happier living with one caring parent than two who are always quarrelling.

Under Pressure Q&A

It's really hurtful — what can I do?

I used to live with my mum but then she got sick and my gran looked after us. But now she can't cope with us all so I'm living with **foster parents**. It's not for long, because Mum's getting better. But some kids in my class say that I'm homeless and that my mum doesn't want me. It's really hurtful — what can I do?

With your friends to support you, explain to these kids exactly what happened to you and how you'd really appreciate their support. Explain that problems like this can happen to anyone and that you hope they don't happen to them. Tell your foster parents, too. They will have experience of helping young people cope with this type of prejudice. Finally, you could also consider speaking to a counsellor, who will be able to give you valuable support through this difficult time.

GENDER DISCRIMINATION

Should girls and boys each behave in a certain way? Do they only have certain abilities and interests? Gender stereotyping says that they do. This can lead to discrimination and prejudice against both genders.

GENDER STEREOTYPING

Gender stereotyping is the belief that, for example, boys can't dance, cook or enjoy creative writing. Or that girls are poor at science, technology and mathematics. None of this is true, but it can mean that boys and girls are not encouraged to use their talents. As adults, they might not find jobs they enjoy.

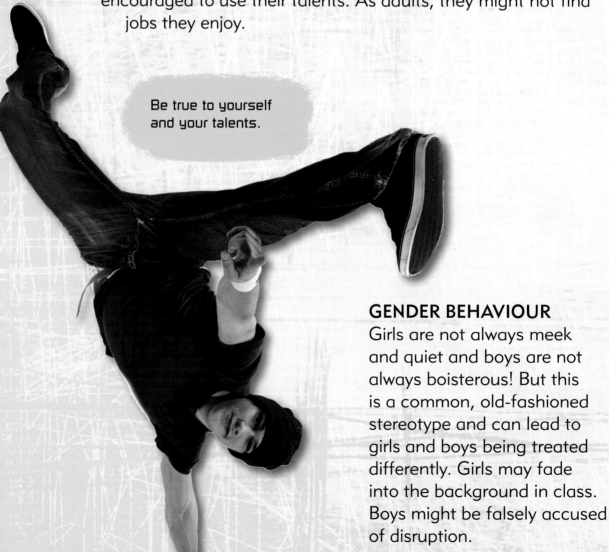

Be true to yourself and your talents.

GENDER BEHAVIOUR

Girls are not always meek and quiet and boys are not always boisterous! But this is a common, old-fashioned stereotype and can lead to girls and boys being treated differently. Girls may fade into the background in class. Boys might be falsely accused of disruption.

TACKLING GENDER STEREOTYPING

If you feel that you are being stereotyped or are treated differently because of your gender, you need to stand up for your rights and challenge the assumptions of whoever is discriminating against you.
If you are being bullied for doing something that some see as not typical for your gender, you need to speak to a trusted teacher or school counsellor about it.

If some activities, such as sports, are not available to both sexes at your school, speak to a teacher about whether this could be changed.

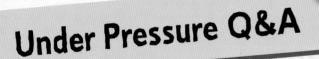

Under Pressure Q&A

How can I change their minds?

My brothers go to boxing classes at a local club. So now there's a new girls' club and some of my friends are going but my parents say boxing's not for girls. It's so unfair! I've watched my brothers training and it's all about keeping fit and thinking ahead, and it's really safe. So what's the problem?

I can see that this is a case of unequal treatment, but your parents are just trying to look out for you. Ask if you can go along to the girls' club and see exactly what goes on. Do not be tempted to disobey your parents by joining in! Explain calmly to your parents the routine at the club and the care they take with the girls' well-being. Ask them politely if they'll come and watch with you. If they still won't agree, maybe the trainer or your friends' parents can put them at ease.

SEXUAL ORIENTATION

Sexual orientation describes who we are attracted to. Men and women are most often attracted to each other. However, some women – lesbians – are attracted to other women. Gay men are attracted to other men. And some people – bisexuals – feel the same way about both. A person might feel that he or she should really be the opposite gender. This is called transgender. Lesbian, gay, bisexual and transgender (LGBT) people can suffer a lot of discrimination and prejudice.

This gay rights march in New York reminds us that discrimination can continue into adulthood.

UNDERSTANDING YOUR FEELINGS
As you get into your teens, you might feel attracted to people of the same sex. Sometimes the feelings don't last into adulthood – sometimes they do. Young people often call others 'gay' to **humiliate** them. This is wrong and childish. Being gay or straight are just types of relationship.

MEDIA DISCRIMINATION

Media and social networking sites can whip up prejudice about the LGBT community. This makes things very hard for young LGBTs, especially at school. There is often media prejudice about LGBT parents, yet statistics show that their children are usually confident and happy.

HELP AND SUPPORT

If you are facing prejudice or bullying that relates to sexual orientation, speak to your school counsellor or phone a helpline for help and support. LGBT youth-support networks such as It Gets Better offer great advice and friendship. If one of your friends is facing this kind of discrimination, don't let him or her suffer alone. Offer him or her your support, and show you know that our sexual orientation is just one part of who we are.

Most helplines can help you get in touch with organizations where other young people understand your problems.

Under Pressure Q&A

They think being gay's a problem — what can I do?

I've got two dads — they're gay — and they're really great. But some of my school friends say they're not normal and they call me gay too. What shall I do? Not everyone behaves like this, and one of my dads is a school governor with other parents. They really like him and don't treat him differently.

Try explaining to the group of boys that there are many types of normal! We are all different in some way; and in most ways, your dads are no different from other parents. The school governors don't bother pointing out any difference and the boys should be more mature. If they continue being rude, hang out with more open-minded friends. Be confident in yourself and your family.

BEING OVERWEIGHT

There is a lot of pressure on young people to be thin. And there is increasing discrimination and prejudice against those who are overweight. These two things can create body-image problems among young people.

Overweight young people who are bullied are likely to feel isolated and unhappy.

FEELING THE PRESSURE

Young people who are overweight often face discrimination and bullying. They may be excluded from activities such as sports, verbally abused and sometimes physically attacked. This can lead to feelings of low self-esteem, anxiety and depression. Sometimes their suffering may lead to **eating disorders** such as **anorexia nervosa**, binge-eating and bulimia.

MEDIA MESSAGES

Media stories and images often demonize people with weight problems. At the same time, they encourage us to copy slim celebrities and to believe that being thin is the ideal. This increases prejudice against those who are overweight. Bear in mind that images of models and actors are often **airbrushed**! And **body doubles** are used in movies, even for major stars.

Avoid comparing yourself or anyone else with models or unreal images of celebrities in magazines.

HOW TO COPE

If you are being discriminated against or bullied for being overweight, don't just accept it. Speak to a teacher or school counsellor if you are being bullied or excluded from activities in school. Remember that there is much more to you than your body shape. However, if you have health concerns about your weight, consult a health professional for a proper assessment. They will check whether you need to lose weight. If you are advised to follow a diet programme, try to find friends who will encourage and support you.

'It really got to me'

I've been overweight since I was about six. For a long time I was okay. But recently it really got to me. The guys at my local football club wouldn't pass me the ball and started pushing me about — which is totally prejudiced of them, because I may be big, but I'm a good player. I felt so bad about myself that I stopped going. Of course that didn't help — I felt completely alone and got much less exercise. So everything got worse. Eventually my sister and I went to the doctor and she — the doctor — asked Mum to take us to a family group to help us all lose weight. Now I'm eating better. I'm still overweight but feel a bit more confident again. And I've joined the school football club now, where people are more friendly.

FASHION AND APPEARANCE

The way you dress and your hairstyle say a lot about you. But there can be a lot of discrimination and prejudice about the way young people choose to look. Criticism and scorn can come from adults as well as peers.

Why follow trends when you could create your own? You could start a blog to give a voice to your own individual style.

UNDER PRESSURE

There's a lot of pressure on young people to follow the latest fashion. But some young people don't want to, while others simply can't afford to. Top brands spend huge amounts of money and use celebrities to boost the popularity and sales of their fashion items. It can be really hard to resist this money-making machine if you face prejudice for not buying in to the latest style.

RESISTING THE PRESSURE

If you feel pressure to buy the latest style but can't afford it, be honest with your friends. If it feels really important to you, maybe buy just one inexpensive item that has this season's colours. But, above all, make sure that it suits you and your personality. If you have a lot of money, be sensitive to friends who don't. Don't become someone who discriminates against those who can't or don't want to follow the latest fashion.

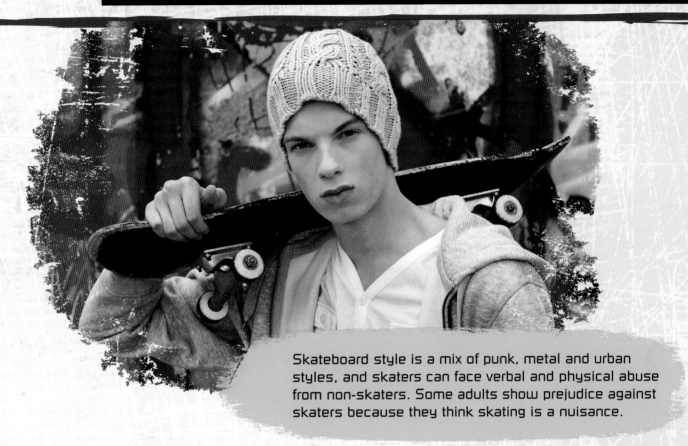

Skateboard style is a mix of punk, metal and urban styles, and skaters can face verbal and physical abuse from non-skaters. Some adults show prejudice against skaters because they think skating is a nuisance.

LOOKING DIFFERENT

Young people with striking styles such as **goth**, cyber goth, **emo** and **punk** often face prejudice. Some even face physical violence. This is against the law and if this happens to you, you should speak to a trusted adult straight away.

Under Pressure Q&A

My friends make jokes about me — what can I do?

I don't have a lot of money so my clothes are often not like the latest fashion and I look really plain. My friends make jokes about me to each other and even to my face. It makes me so depressed that I don't bother much about how I look any more. What can I do?

Real friends would not make hurtful jokes, so speak to them and explain how their prejudice is making you feel. It sounds like your friends are into following the latest fashions. Instead of trying to keep up with them, why don't you create your own style? You could learn to adapt the clothes you already have or cheap charity-shop finds. There are many websites, blogs and online tutorials about alternative fashion. Be proud of your own style and what it says about you!

JOBS AND WEALTH

Some young people face prejudice about the jobs their parents or carers do, or about whether their family is poor or rich. If this is happening to you, you will want to defend and support your family. Educating others is the key.

Many jobs help to build our communities.

ATTITUDES TO JOBS AND MONEY

Some people consider certain jobs to be 'better' than others. But all jobs teach us valuable skills, such as teamwork, concentration and punctuality. Many low-paid jobs keep our environment clean and healthy and our elderly cared for. Many higher-paid jobs help companies and organizations run smoothly. We could not do without either kind. Yet many young people suffer prejudice because of the work their parents do or how much money their family has.

HOW TO VALUE WORK

If you are quick to be prejudiced against certain jobs, think about how those jobs contribute to society, and respect the skills and effort they require. Don't focus on your friends' money, or lack of money. Young people from wealthy families can also suffer prejudice, which is often based on jealousy.

OUT OF WORK

Young people can also face enormous prejudice if their parents or carers are out of work. Politicians and the media sometimes **stigmatize** those without jobs. If you face prejudice or discrimination because your parent is unemployed, challenge those who are targeting you. Make it clear that anyone can lose their job. In some towns and cities, work is difficult to find, however hard people try.

It's easy to think that money is the most important thing. But young people from wealthy families can also face prejudice.

Under Pressure Q&A

Why don't they respect my dad's job?

My dad had a really good job. He was an IT manager. Then he lost his job because the company he worked for had to close down. Dad couldn't find another IT job so now he is working as a labourer until he finds something in IT. The neighbours are okay about it except for the kids, who I used to play with. Now they laugh at me, especially as I can't have all the things I used to. Why can't they respect him?

Your dad is one of hundreds of thousands of people who have lost their jobs in recent years. But you should be proud of your dad and his job. He is working hard for the family and he will be learning valuable skills because all jobs teach us a lot. You can tell your neighbours' kids this.

DISABILITY DISCRIMINATION

Young people with physical or learning disabilities, or mental-health issues, can suffer terrible prejudice and discrimination. This can range from being patronized or being excluded from activities to physical and emotional bullying.

Talking with trusted people can help with mental-health issues. Online networks especially for young people give great support, too.

LEARNING ABOUT DISABILITY

Discriminating against people with disabilities, and their families, is cowardly and ignorant. All of us have a range of talents and abilities, as well as things we can't do so well. Rather than getting hung up on those things that people can't do, focus on what they *can* do – their skills, talents and interests.

DEALING WITH DISCRIMINATION

If you have a disability and are being excluded from activities, make sure that the people who are leaving you out know exactly how you can participate, or what they need to do for you to be able to join in. Hopefully they will learn from this and be more inclusive in future. If you or someone that you know are being bullied because of a disability, you must speak to a trusted adult. If this is happening in school, speak to a teacher or counsellor.

HIGHLIGHT A HERO

Don't make assumptions! Disability is no obstacle to success. President Franklin D Roosevelt (1882–1945) was disabled. In 1963, Stephen Hawking was diagnosed with motor neurone disease and given two years to live – and yet he has become one of the world's greatest scientists. Baroness Tanni Grey-Thompson won 11 Paralympic Gold medals and is now an important political voice against discrimination.

'I left the other boys behind!'

I can't walk properly because one of my legs is amputated from above the knee. It's because I got sick with meningitis when I was little. It can happen to anyone. When I started secondary school, other boys wouldn't let me join in their games. Some said I might get hurt and a few called me horrible names. Then last term my class went to the climbing wall at the local leisure centre. I've been climbing there with Dad since I was four. So I shot up to the ceiling and left the other boys behind! Some of the guys started hanging out with me after that. I can swim faster than them, too, and dive from the top board. The really mean guys are now jealous so I just hang out with the friendly ones.

Clubs for disabled people offer leadership skills as well as a range of activities.

ACHIEVEMENT

Some students struggle with schoolwork, or maybe just a particular subject. This can lead to discrimination from their peers, particularly if they're moved to a special class. High-achieving students can also be discriminated against and often face jealousy and isolation.

Develop all your talents and try out different skills. It will help you understand what you are good at and also that you can't be good at everything!

MAKING THINGS WORSE

Struggling with schoolwork is made much worse by discrimination and taunts. This can lead to students becoming depressed, anxious or disruptive, and sometimes missing school. If they miss regular classes and any extra study groups, it is even harder for them to do well.

HOW TO COPE

If you are suffering from thoughtless taunts and are being shunned, teachers should be involved in sorting it out. They will be keen to uphold school policies on inclusion, which means treating students equally, whatever their capabilities. Teachers can help to make bullies understand that they are behaving in an ignorant, disrespectful way.

DON'T GET STEREOTYPED!

If you need help with one or two subjects, other students might think you struggle with everything. Make it clear that you are good at some things but not at others – like most people! Are those who stereotype you good at everything? Are they as good as you at your best subject or sport? Take pride in your achievements. If you have a hobby or sport outside school that you excel at, let them know about it.

SMART BUT ISOLATED

Smart students often face name-calling and isolation from fellow students. Again, this is something that is best tackled with the help of teachers or school mentors. Try to get support from other students in your position, too, and maybe hang out with them.

Museums and galleries can inspire you if you're feeling a bit down about your studies. Some institutions offer challenging Saturday classes for high achievers.

Under Pressure Q&A

Do I have to get lower grades to keep my friends?

I want to do well at school so I work hard, but I get blanked by my friends when I do. When I get good marks, they call me a 'geek'. I pretend not to mind, but it's really upsetting. I'm starting to mess up my work a bit and get lower grades, but I don't think that's the answer. How can I keep my friends? I'm really miserable.

First of all, tell your friends how hurtful you find this treatment. Point out that they do things well that you can't — that you admire them for their talents and wouldn't dream of teasing them about their skills. Speak to your teachers or parents about what's going on, too. If things don't get any better, you could try to find new friends who share your goals or who are less judgemental of others.

WHERE YOU COME FROM

It can sometimes be hard to fit in at school because you live in a particular part of town. Your neighbourhood might have a reputation for crime or poverty, or seem very smart but unwelcoming to outsiders. Either way, you can experience prejudice and discrimination. Your accent often signals where you are from — bullies may pick on your accent if it is different from theirs.

These young people are clearing up their run-down streets. Your actions and voice can change negative opinions and overturn prejudice in your community.

STICK UP FOR THE GOOD

Stereotyping and prejudice can affect the aims and achievements of young people living in a particular area. If people are prejudiced about the area you come from, remember that all areas have their good and bad points. Get to know your area and stick up for the good things about it and the great people who live there. You could join a community development project that is aimed at young people and try to get media interest in what you do.

'People often link accents and intelligence in their minds. This is partly because TV and radio presenters often sound stereotypically 'educated'.

'They don't criticize my choice of friends any more'

I go around with three really close friends from school. After school we belong to the same clubs too, like gymnastics — and we go swimming. But Mum and Dad said my friends are no good for me because they live on a really poor housing estate and they don't speak like us. I didn't know what to do. Then I spent my pocket money on some cakes and asked my friends back to my house after school. Mum looked furious but my friends were lovely and very polite — because they always are! So things are much better now and Mum and Dad don't criticize my choice of friends any more.

THE WAY WE SOUND

Our accents can tell everyone where we're from but say nothing about who we are. Unfortunately, stereotypes have grown around accents. Some are thought to show which social class you come from and how smart you are.

DON'T LOSE WHO YOU ARE

If people find fault with your accent, ask them why accents are so important to them. You'll find plenty of examples of interesting and high-achieving adults with your accent. Don't forget — if you lose your accent you also lose part of who you are!

AGE DISCRIMINATION

People of all age groups are guilty of showing age discrimination. This can be made worse by media prejudice. For example, young people can be stereotyped as uncaring, rude and lazy. The elderly may be portrayed as feeble-minded, with outdated ideas and nothing to offer society.

NEGATIVE STEREOTYPES

If you think adults have negative stereotypes about you, talk to them about how you feel. For example, adults often think that teenagers are lazy because they stay in bed later. In fact, research shows that young people's bodies follow a different rhythm of sleeping and waking than adults. Discussing things in a friendly way will help you to find compromises.

WORKPLACE DISCRIMINATION

Online youth forums show that employers often discriminate against young jobseekers. Some employers believe that young people have poor time-keeping and lazy attitudes. If you think that you have been discriminated against, there are free advice organizations that can help you.

You will find a lot of blogs about youth discrimination. But don't forget that young people are not the only age group to face prejudice.

SHOW YOUR WORTH

Even if you're too young to work, build up skills that show how competent and mature you are. Many businesses lack employees with up-to-date computer skills, which is where you might shine. Doing voluntary work and raising money for charities will also help your chances.

You could help document the lives of elderly people for a local community website. This will show how much you value their experiences.

CHANGING ATTITUDES

Practical activities help to change stereotypes. If you want to tackle age discrimination, you could take part in a supervised community scheme to help the elderly. This will challenge prejudice against the young by proving that you are caring and active. It's possible that listening and talking to the elderly members of your community might change some of your assumptions about the elderly, too.

'It's just because we're young'

Me and my friends were hanging out outside the local sweet shop but the guy who runs it kept telling us to go away. He said we made too much noise and put other customers off. It's just because we're young. He even put a notice up that only two teenagers could go in at once. And we spend money in there every day! We were really mad and made extra noise outside so he called the community policewoman. The policewoman watched us and said we were blocking the shop door and that some little kids and older people looked frightened. So we agreed to stand well to the side. It's a bit better now with the shop owner.

AVOIDING PATTERNS OF PREJUDICE

Our attitudes can be easily influenced by other people. Most of us are led in some way by parents and other family members, or community, religious and social groups. Sometimes we learn patterns of prejudice that are hard to shake off. But it's important to break habits that harm others and, eventually, ourselves.

LISTEN TO OTHERS
Try to mix with people from as many different backgrounds as you can. It's a good idea to listen to all points of view. When speaking to others about stereotyping or prejudice, discuss your ideas in a calm, friendly way with those who might not agree with you.

WE'RE ALL INDIVIDUALS
Being prejudiced about others damages us as much as them. Try to focus on treating each person as an individual. Remember that others will have hopes, dreams and talents, just like you. When we make mistakes about someone, we should be big enough to say sorry.

If friends or peers are leaving someone out, challenge their prejudice and don't become part of their discrimination.

JEALOUSY AND PREJUDICE

It's easy to feel insecure about your friendships. You might feel pushed out by a new member of your group and be tempted to discriminate against them. Build your confidence by developing the things you're good at. We can all be unsure about ourselves from time to time. Use this understanding to welcome others.

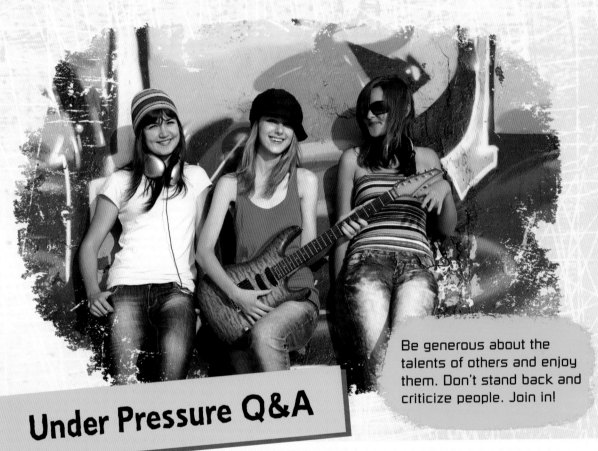

Be generous about the talents of others and enjoy them. Don't stand back and criticize people. Join in!

Under Pressure Q&A

Why am I being so mean?

My best friend wants to bring in another friend but I don't want to upset what we two have. This other girl is really smart and comes from a nice neighbourhood — she's got an indoor pool and everything. And she's got her own dress style, which everyone says is amazing. But I've never liked her, because I feel like she makes me look stupid and uncool. I keep trying to persuade my friend that this girl's a show-off and a swot and looks a mess, but then when I'm by myself I cry because I don't like what I'm doing. Why am I being so mean?

Your behaviour makes me think you are feeling insecure about your own personality and gifts. This is making you prejudiced against the new girl, as well as the other people that you target for being good at things. Your best friend obviously sees all the good things about you. So you must, too! However, also try to find something in common with the new girl and praise her talents if you can. If you can stop being so prejudiced, you will start to feel much better about yourself.

THINK FOR YOURSELF

Discrimination and prejudice in newspaper headlines and gossip columns, and on TV, radio and the internet bombard us daily. It's very hard to stand back and ask ourselves what we think is true and fair. Stories are often exaggerated to attract viewers and listeners, and money from advertisers.

You'll often find new friends if you support those facing discrimination or prejudice.

KEEP A LEVEL HEAD

Media stories can stir up trouble and make young people feel discriminated against, even if they've never thought about it before. If you've always felt confident about yourself and your background and you have a wide group of friends, don't allow media stories to spoil this. Trust yourself and your friends. Remember, the media thrives on division and conflict!

MAKE UP YOUR OWN MIND

News stories might target, for example, someone's religion or people from a certain country. Don't always believe the story, especially if it's from the internet or social media, because these are often based on opinion rather than fact. Listen to local community leaders or other responsible adults, learn the facts and make up your own mind.

Why not turn off your mobile and internet for a few hours a week and instead do something fun with your friends?

LIVE IN THE REAL WORLD

Blogs and other social media are fun, but they can be harmful, too. If a blogger attacks someone, make sure you don't agree with his or her criticism just to make yourself popular. Stop and think about what they have written. Does it sound as if the blogger's views are based on prejudice? Also, remember that online comments have real-life consequences for the person being attacked.

Under Pressure Q&A

Isn't that just free speech?

Sometimes I see things on news blogs that trash people because of how they look or where they're from. I don't always agree with them but it's just their opinion. And isn't that just free speech?

Firstly, it is never okay to hurt people. We shouldn't think that our opinions are so important that others will always want to know them. In the long run, thoughtful, helpful advice is respected more than prejudice and criticism. Mature people learn when to hold back. Free speech is a right that should help people, not harm them.

THE WAY FORWARD

The way forward for all of us is to be more open-minded. We need to get to know people for who they are and not believe stereotypes about their origins or circumstances.

Learn more about others through clubs, debating societies and blogs.

IMPROVING YOUR SELF-WORTH

If you are facing discrimination or bullying as a result of prejudice, you may feel very low. Boost your confidence by spending time with supportive, like-minded friends, family members and youth support teams. Speak to a teacher or school counsellor to tackle the bullying. If you find it hard to speak to someone face-to-face, you could phone a helpline for advice. Also, try to to expand your life beyond school. Becoming involved in community activities or voluntary work will help you to meet people who share your values and interests.

SPEAK OUT!

Make sure you support those suffering discrimination and prejudice. If you feel you can't do this on your own, then find friends who will back you up. You'll be surprised how many people secretly share your views. Get inspiration from teen blogs and support networks. Remember that there are laws against discrimination and prejudice that will back you up.

AROUND THE WORLD

Prejudice doesn't just affect how we think about people in our own neighbourhood – it affects how we think about the rest of the world, too. Many young people in other countries have not had the same chances in life as you. Sometimes you may feel that you don't care, because of poor attitudes towards the countries they are from. Remember that these people have the same dreams as you.

We can learn a lot from people in other parts of the world. This helps stop stereotyping and prejudice.

'We should have reached out to the new kids'

I live in a small town and we all know each other and there haven't been many newcomers. But six months ago, a big tech company set up about 20 kilometres away. So now there are families in town that aren't like us and lots are even from other countries. We gave some of the kids a hard time at school. Then the tech company invited us kids to their complex — it was amazing! And they told us what kinds of jobs the new kids' parents do and how they all want to give something good to the area. Things have got a bit better at school. But actually I think we should have reached out to the new kids and not just left it to the company.

GLOSSARY

airbrushed Altered an image to make it more attractive.

anorexia nervosa A serious eating disorder in which the fear of weight gain leads to eating very little and extreme weight loss.

anxiety Fear about something that might happen and your ability to cope with it.

assumptions Ideas or opinions that people believe to be true without proof.

body doubles People who stand in for actors or models in films and magazines.

bulimia A serious eating disorder in which a person overeats then forces him or herself to vomit.

depression A mental state marked by sadness, inactivity and lack of self-esteem.

disruptive Causing a disturbance by interrupting the normal progress of something.

eating disorders Emotional conditions that cause eating habits that are not normal, such as anorexia.

emo A style that may include wearing tight jeans and having long black hair. Emos are supposed to be emotional and sensitive.

ethnic group People of the same race or nationality.

extremism Holding very strong opinions on something and often believing in very strong action.

foster parents Adults who look after a child who cannot be cared for by his or her birth parents.

goth A style that includes wearing black clothes and black and white make-up.

humiliate Make someone feel stupid and ashamed, especially in front of other people.

identity Who you are.

illegal Against the law.

punk A style that may include wearing metal chains, leather clothes and having brightly coloured hair.

racism A belief that some races are better than others; a dislike of a certain race or people from a certain country.

refugee A person who has been forced to leave their country or home, because there is a war or for political, religious or social reasons.

scroungers People who live off others and do not work for what they have.

self-esteem A person's belief in his or her own worth and abilities.

shun Turn your back on someone and ignore him or her.

stigmatize Describe or regard someone with great disapproval.

suspended Sent away from school for a certain period.

WEBSITES

www.dosomething.org/
This discussion forum also shows you how to take action against discrimination.

www.goodreads.com/group/show/59835-teens-against-discrimination
A teen website and blog campaign against discrimination and prejudice.

www.itgetsbetter.org
The website of It Gets Better, a programme dedicated to helping LGBT teens and others who are bullied.

www.un.org/cyberschoolbus/discrim/id_8_ud_race.asp
This website helps to explain and tackle discrimination and bullying.

www.youngminds.org.uk
A UK charity committed to improving the emotional wellbeing and mental health of children and young people.

www.yre.org.uk/about.html
The website of Youth Against Racism in Europe.

HELPLINES

Childline 0800 1111 www.childline.org.uk

Samaritans 08457 90 90 90 www.samaritans.org

SupportLine 01708 765200 www.supportline.org.uk

BOOKS

NON-FICTION

Bullying Michele Elliot, Hodder Children's Books, 2005

Bullying: How to Deal with Taunting, Teasing and Tormenting, Kathleen Winkler, Enslow, 2005

Discrimination, Greenhaven Press, 2014

FICTION

Billy Elliot, Melvin Burgess (based on Lee Hall's motion picture screenplay), Chicken House, 2001

Neither This Nor That, Aliya Husain, lulu.com, 2010

INDEX